Being a Queen

in the

KINGDOM

Keondria Knox

Thank You

First and foremost always, thanks be to my Lord and Savior Jesus Christ who trusted me to birth this assignment. I never knew writing a book would be a part of my own story but with Him, through Him, and in Him it came to fruition. I need to thank my amazing husband who has been my constant "pusher". We've seen tough days but thanks be to God who allowed us to now be living our best days. I love you babe! Fifteen years is a long time but not nearly long enough. Let's keep this thing going forever. To my beautiful daughters who encouraged me through their excitement to read the final product. "Mama, I know we're not married but can we read your book?" Their anticipation gave me an even greater purpose to see this to the end. Finally, to every wife I have had the pleasure of personally observing. Some of the most significant lessons were learned from just watching you live your lives. Some taught me what to do in my marriage and some taught me what not to do. Either way, the lessons I learned from you made me a better wife. So thank you!

Jewels *of* Wisdom

Preface

Ever wonder why there are so many failing marriages, especially in the body of Christ? It's simple. We have abandoned the manufacturer's guide and adopted the world's standard for marriage. Marriage was instituted, created, and ordained by God. In Mark 10:6-9 Jesus says "But from the beginning of the creation God made them male and female. For this cause shall a man leave his father and mother, and cleave to his wife; And they twain shall be one flesh: so then they are no more twain, but one flesh. What therefore God hath joined together, let not man put asunder". Marriage is a God thing. An amazingly beautiful God thing! So how can we flourish in this amazing God thing if we deviate from God's master plan concerning it?

Whatever God has Satan wants too. Because God created marriage, the enemy has created his own version of what marriage should be and tries to trick us to believe that his way is okay. This has been going on in the body of Christ for much too long. I believe that if we as Christians get it right and begin to live out our marriages based on Kingdom standards, we can become lighthouses of righteous marriages for the world to pattern.

This book was birthed from my God-given vision and desire to help wives in the body of Christ understand the magnitude of their role as wives in the Kingdom. I have been married for fifteen years. I don't profess to know everything. But what I do know is that without God my marriage would be non-existent today.

This is the most transparent I have ever been with my marriage. I share our beginning and some of our trials that lead to our separation; but, I also share our story of restoration. I've learned so many things during my marriage from personal experience, but there are some things I discuss that I haven't personally experienced but have witnessed the effects from others' relationships. What I found out is that we, as wives, don't fully understand our roles and more importantly, how significant our role is as queen.

1 Peter 2:9 tells us that we are "a chosen race, royal priesthood". We are royalty! It's time for us to stop living beneath who God said we are. At first thought, this book may seem to be one-sided; and quite frankly, it is. What I mean

is that it strictly and unequivocally focuses on the role of the wife-the queen.

I can guarantee that many times while you're reading this you will say "but the reason I did that is because he did this" or "his actions don't line up with being treated as a king so why should I do that". I challenge you to take a moment before beginning the first chapter to make a decision to have an open heart and mind. Early on in my marriage, I struggled with not only understanding the power that I possessed and the change I could create in my home but also knowing what my role is and submitting to it.

So, every queen deserves jewels, right? Well this book details fifteen jewels of wisdom I have accumulated in my fifteen year marriage to my king. Before we begin, let's decide now that for the duration of our time together, we'll hit the pause button on the Blame Game. Some of us have been playing that game since we got married and are the reigning champions. Instead, let's choose to will ourselves past the pointing fingers stage and be receptive to fully accepting our role. The only way we will be able to do that is by inviting God into the situation. So, pray this prayer with me:

Father, I thank you for this opportunity to learn and grow in you. Thank you for your divine wisdom, your amazing grace, and your overwhelming love that has encompassed me all these years. I take this moment to ask for forgiveness for all the times I was less than what you called me to be as a wife. I surrender my whole self to you right now. I open my heart and mind to receive what is for me. I thank you and love you, in the precious name of Jesus Christ, Amen.

Jewel #1

Never Forget Your Beginning

"Whoso findeth a wife findeth a good *thing*, and obtaineth favour of the LORD." Proverbs 18:22 KJV

Our girls love to hear the story about how Cortney and I first met so I'll share it with you. They love how animated my delivery is but I'll dial it back a bit for you guys.

So anyone who knows me knows I have a deep love for Chick-Fil-A. Aside from the food and service being impeccable, it was my very first job. The best part, however, is that it was the place I met the most handsome, caramel-skinned boy I had ever seen. I came into work one afternoon and saw him at one of the food court tables talking to my manager. I was only sixteen at the time. Listen, I was what the old folks would call "smitten".

I think it's important to mention that my manager and I were very close. We went to church together and he had known me my whole life, so I had confidence that I could persuade him to hire this guy. Now, I don't know if he hired him just for my sake or if he was actually impressed with his interview. I really don't care how it happened, I'm just glad it did!

This guy comes in and changes the entire trajectory of my life. I remember seeing him for the first time and knowing that we would be something to each other. At that point, I didn't know that we would one day get married but I did know we would mean something to each other. Is that what love at first sight is? I don't know, but that's how I felt.

So, we became friends but there was definitely a mutual attraction there that exceeded friendship. We were both in relationships with other people so we didn't immediately start dating. We were only sixteen at the time but we both felt that those were pretty important relationships.

Anyway, I was promoted at work, which was great because I now had the responsibility of making the schedule. Normally, I worked the day shift and he worked the night shift. But guess what I did as soon as I got promoted? Yes, I started working more night shifts. Looking back on it, I was kind of thirsty, huh? Don't judge me!

So time passed and we started hanging out together with mutual friends from work but we never pursued each other because we were already dating other people. Little did I know we wouldn't have many other chances to hang out. My sister and I had to move out of state to live with our dad. I was so disappointed and sad. I thought for sure that was the end of our friendship. I decided that on my last day of work I would give him my phone number. Well, he didn't come in that day, so I gave it to my manager to give to him. A couple days later, I was gone.

I think I was in Alabama for about two weeks and I still hadn't heard from him. One Saturday I heard the phone ringing. My sister answers the phone and says, "yeah, sure, hold on". Then she leans over to me with a big stupid grin on her face and whispers "it's for you, it's Cortney". I could have fallen through the floor! I was so shocked and excited and nervous! He actually called me, I didn't think he would. I mean he had a girlfriend! So after I got feeling back in my hands, I grabbed the phone and began the amazing journey of Cortney & Keondria.

As you can imagine, our relationship grew quickly. I had never loved any person on this earth more than I loved Cortney Knox. He loved me, took care of me, encouraged me, and most importantly, he loved the Lord. We connected on so many levels. When I first met him I realized how different he was from other guys I knew. His response to situations was different. He would talk to me about things like his first time experiencing the power of God. We were only sixteen! And although I had been in church my entire life, for me, that wasn't the normal conversation for a guy his age to discuss with a girl he liked. He was just different!

I didn't stay in Alabama for long because we just couldn't stand being that far away from each other. Our relationship had blossomed into something so beautiful in such a short time. It was built on love and mutual respect for one another. I remember him being so protective of me. All he wanted was for me to be happy and I wanted the same for him. We were best friends. We laughed, talked all night, made plans for our future; disobeyed our parents to spend more time together (listen, pray for me because I have to reap that); we were all about each other. We were poised for a fairytale life but…real life happened.

Jewel #2

Lose the Religion

"And Jesus answered and said unto him, Get thee
behind me, Satan: for it is written, Thou shalt worship
the Lord thy God, and Him only shalt thou serve."
Luke 4:8 KJV

I was reared in a devout Pentecostal church from birth. There were certain traditions and teachings that we had to abide by. Women couldn't wear pants, we didn't celebrate holidays, and there were no women ministers or pastors, to name a few. One teaching discouraged us from dating outside of our church. And it's my understanding that, if you did date outside of the church, you should have the intention of drawing them in, not the other way around.

I didn't know much about other denominations or churches in general because we never visited other churches. Most of my comprehension at that time in my life was what I now know to be religion and not relationship with Jesus. Religion is a "personal set of religious attitudes, beliefs, and practices". I thought I knew Jesus, but in actuality I just knew about Him. I never grasped the concept of having a true relationship with Him. I understood more about the rules and practices of my church than the standards and principles of God's Word. There is a huge difference between having a true personal relationship and being religious.

Cortney came from a non-denominational church. He would talk to me about things that escaped my understanding. He would tell me about things God spoke to him, and that was just the most foreign concept to me. God spoke to you? What? If I'm being honest, I really didn't believe him. I would just smile and nod. I didn't even want to have those conversations because I knew we would have differing opinions. I didn't want to have an argument. I was deeply rooted in my "religion". I knew it to be the truth-the only truth. I loved him and didn't want to jeopardize our relationship by arguing over "church stuff", so I just didn't go there!

Needless to say, our relationship grew into something very serious. When I say serious, I mean getting knocked up serious! The night I discovered I was pregnant was easily one of the scariest moments in my entire life. The weight of having to care for another human being at that point in my life was unimaginable. I was in total shock. I compulsively took three tests just to be sure. When I was sure that I was sure I called Cortney over. He came shortly after I called probably just thinking I wanted to see him. He had no idea the bomb I was about to drop. I answered the door to a smile and an endearing kiss- all the while knowing I was about to deliver the most devastating blow of his life. The pit in my stomach was sinking to deeper levels by the second.

I asked him to sit down and I pulled out the three sticks. A look of total confusion washed over his face. His intelligence must've temporarily vanished because he said, "what dat mean?" I'm yelling in my head "YOU KNOW WHAT THAT MEANS!!" But I didn't verbalize my frustration. I explained everything and as soon as he saw the panic in my eyes his demeanor completely shifted. He started consoling me. I knew he was dealing with his own inner emotions but he shelved his feelings to comfort me. He was confident and fearless. He reassured me that everything would be fine. Then for a while, we just sat in silence as I laid on his shoulder. A million thoughts swarmed through my mind as I laid there. After a while we both regained the mental capacity to start back talking.

We came up with a plan of how we were going to tell our parents. I think we waited a week or so before telling everyone. What I didn't know is that after Cortney left me that night, he went home and prayed. We're seventeen, living at home with parents (in my case, living with a family friend), and pregnant. What in the world were we to do?

So he went home and as he begins to pray while pacing the floor of his bedroom, the Holy Spirit says "'Do you love her?' Do I love her? With a look of indignation he whispered, 'Yes, I love her!' 'Well marry her'". He thought, MARRY HER? We are seventeen, I'm still in school, people will talk about me! Excuses flooded his mind.

Cortney's first response was going to Jesus; my first response was going to my spiritual leader. I remember going and telling him about everything and about our decision to get married. With any situation in my life, be it big or small, I would run to my leader. That was my immediate response. Needless to say, because of the rules of our church, he explained to me that he couldn't support my decision. Cortney was not a member of the church. He even warned me against it. I pretty much knew that would be the response but I still left out of that office feeling hurt and disappointed.

Cortney had already found us a house to rent; he'd paid deposit and renovation costs. So he was excited to tell his pastors about our decision. To his surprise they tried to pay him to not marry me. "Oh, she's Pentecostal?? Haha, it'll never work!" Let me clarify them trying to pay him. They wanted to reimburse him for any money that he had already spent towards our house.

So here we are, in the most difficult time of our lives. We were youngsters just yearning for the approval, validation, guidance, and encouragement of our spiritual leaders. Their response was essentially for us to walk away from the relationship. End it and we'll help you get through it on the back end. We knew that was not the answer! We had no choice but to surrender to the Holy Spirit.

My mother in love was the only voice of support we had. She knew that she had raised Cortney to have a relationship with God for himself so she trusted that when he said he heard from Him it was real. She definitely had her doubts and fears but ultimately she trusted the

God in the son she'd raised to lean and depend on Him. She was really a great encouragement to us. She told us that God ordained family from the beginning. So it's His desire for family to be whole and strong, not to be separated.

Cortney knew without a shadow of doubt that God spoke to him so that's what he stood on. We started to get excited about beginning our journey. He had no trouble at all finding that house. He took pride in being able to provide for his little family. It seemed as if the hand of the Lord was on us because everything came rather easily. Even with us being only seventeen we didn't have trouble getting the things we wanted. Cort always says that because we made the decision to do things the way God intended (getting married), He began to open doors for us and bless us in ways that no one else could. He caused people we didn't even know to be a blessing to us.

Because of the law, we had to wait until we were eighteen to get married, which was not far off. I remember being so happy to be married. I loved everything about it. I loved being pregnant. I loved being able to say "my husband". I loved cooking, cleaning, ironing, and just taking care of my husband. It was like a fairytale. We didn't have everything we wanted or the best of everything but we had each other. We were so happy and in love.

Let's fast forward a bit to a year and a half into our marriage. Things started to get a little rocky, then a little shaky, then everything started to crumble all around us. When you actually start living life in the same space as someone, their true selves began to be revealed. The non-support of my leaders and church family really started to affect my marriage.

Church was very important to me. My leaders, family, and friends were important to me. I would be at church sometimes until late at night. I would do things for the church without discussing it with Cort. I didn't discuss it because I knew he had an issue with them not supporting our marriage. Although my words said something different, my actions proved that my leaders and the church came first and my family second. I was sure that everything I was doing at church was the right thing because I was doing God's work! Listen to me, I was full of RELIGION! It made me an insubmissive fool. Religion was me listening to or being bound by a man's view of what my marriage should be and not following God's plan for my life as a wife.

Cortney had already left his church following the leading of the Lord. My mother in love was called into pastoralship around this same time so he decided that he would join. I thought "well he can go to his church and I'll just go to my church. We're both making church a priority-everything will be great!" I visited his church from time to time but I knew that I would never join. I was completely oblivious to the fact that if my leaders didn't accept him or even support our marriage there was no way we would last.

My teachings were that I was not to be in connection with anyone outside of the church. Because that had been embedded in me since before I can remember, I was subconsciously unable to submit to my husband. Real life issues starting arising and decisions had to be made. Now, because Cortney's opinions were different than mine or different than what my leaders were saying, all of a sudden he's not qualified to be the head of our house. All of a sudden, his protective nature that I loved so much became his controlling nature that I refused to be subjected to.

I only moved when my leaders said to move. I put their word above everything! That's all I knew. That was just the way I lived. So when I got married, nothing changed. Traveling out of town to church meetings and not consulting my husband, neglecting to take care of home first.

Of course I now know how out of order I was. But in that moment, I felt justified. I mean, I was churching not clubbing! Looking back and taking an assessment of that time in my life, I wasn't reading and studying the Word for myself. I was not being led by the Holy Spirit because I wasn't even aware that the Holy Spirit could lead me. I had no idea that He would talk to me directly. I never had to actually use my faith in life. If I needed answers, direction, counsel, I went to my leaders.

Let me be clear, I do believe that leadership is essential in life. Everyone needs a pastor. Hebrews 13:17 says "Obey your leaders and do what they say. They are watching over your souls as those who will give an account". However, anyone or anything that takes the place of God in your life has now become your idol. The thing you give first priority to is what you worship. That is not God's will for any of our lives. Without even realizing it my leaders had become my idols. I reverenced them to the point of not even knowing how to have a relationship with God for myself.

When I married Cortney I was so in love with him and just so happy to be his wife. But I had no idea of how hard it would be to sustain a marriage. I was just not prepared to fight through the tough days. And not having a personal relationship with Jesus made the struggle impossible to overcome.

So time passed and with every passing day Cort and I grew further apart. He had to endure a lot during that time. He was disrespected, not just by me but by people close to me who felt like they had a voice in our marriage. Listen, Cortney was not perfect. He made mistakes and didn't do everything he should as a husband, but without a doubt, that time in our lives was on me. It took me a while to be able to admit that truth. I simply needed deliverance!

Our marriage wasn't all bad though. We loved each other and we did do some things right. The major struggles came when Cortney felt a different way than me when it came to certain things as it related to ministry. If we could omit the church differences we experienced in our first years, I believe our marriage wouldn't have been so tumultuous. What do you do when the very thing that is supposed to encourage you is what is tearing you down? When the very people who are supposed to cultivate you are the ones squeezing the life out of you? What do you do?

Cortney was fed up, I was fed up. So we decided to separate. We were separated for six looonnnng months. Do you know how much can happen in six months? That was the darkest time in my life. I was so lost and confused and ashamed. What had happened to our fairytale? We both still loved each other so much. We just couldn't figure out how to make it work. How could our love story end so tragically? I'm over here doing what I want and Cort is over there doing his own thing. There was such a void feeling in my life. Even though I was "free", I felt absolutely empty.

After maybe the fifth month of separation, I remember calling him trying to work things out, but of course he was not having it. I had put him through too much. I had allowed other people to speak recklessly about him. I had torn him down bit by bit, emotionally and mentally. I took a peg out of him every time I made him feel that the words of my leaders trumped his word, every time my mouth got a little too reckless during an argument, every time I swept the subtle disrespectful words from family and friends under the rug. All of those were times I made him feel less than a king in our home.

Ladies, whether we realize or not, things we may feel are small and think doesn't affect our husbands, in reality just reinforces his own insecurities. Insecurities that he masks every day because he wants to appear to be "the man". Over time we can disregard him or his feelings so much until he doesn't know how to be the man because we've made him feel like he's not worthy to hold that place. So I really couldn't blame Cort for not jumping at the thought of a reunion.

I remember feeling like I had really messed everything up. Our daughter would grow up in a single family home, just like I did. I had completely destroyed my chances of living forever with the guy of my dreams. I think I cried every single night for a month straight. I realize now that the problem rested in the fact that I didn't have a personal relationship with Jesus. I was saved but living in and bound by religion. I knew and believed Jesus died for my sins and rose again. I knew him to be my Savior but He wasn't my Lord. The intimacy with Jesus that I have today, I never experienced until I received deliverance. I knew a lot of scriptures-had to memorize them as a child. But I was not allowing the Word to penetrate my heart and change my life. I had to be delivered from religion and from people. There was absolutely no way I could be a good wife if I didn't have personal relationship.

I knew what I needed to do to fix our marriage but my flesh could not, would not let me take that step. It was at my lowest moment when the Holy Spirit spoke to me. He told me to do whatever it took to get my husband back. That was the first time I recognized that God was speaking to me. And I knew exactly what He meant. I did not want to do it-I didn't know how to do it! But I obeyed God. It was then that I made the decision to disconnect from my church. My beloved church, where all my family and friends were, where I had been brought up since birth.

This was absolutely one of the most difficult things I have ever had to do. Relationships begin to die; people started treating me differently-people who were close to me. I literally had to abruptly cut ties with some people because it was hindering not only my relationship with my husband but more importantly my relationship with God.

God used Cort and our separation to deliver me from a life of bondage that had me conformed to placing limits on our limitless God. In order for me to hear God, my flesh had to die. He reached me at my lowest point. He had to show me that He had been speaking to me all along but the voice of people was just louder than His voice.

Before I met Cortney, I was perfectly fine living the life I was accustomed to. But since the day I got delivered, I have not regretted my decision to truly follow Jesus. And being the great God He is, He even restored some relationships with family and friends.

One of the most amazing things about our Savior is that He promised to never leave us. That was his promise to His people. Although we were out of the will of God by having premarital sex and I was not following God's standard for being a wife, God never left us. His grace was sufficient enough to allow us time to get things in order. He allowed us enough time to make a decision that we wanted His way and not ours. God is most faithful in the messy situations created by our hands. So no matter what we do in life, no matter how messed up we are or how screwed up we think our marriage is, God is waiting for our invitation into the situation.

He didn't give Cort the solution he expected when He told him to marry me, but I'm so thankful for his obedience. Cort's obedience gave way to my deliverance. I went from living a religious, mundane life to living a life directed by Jesus Christ, the master orchestrator! I am now fully committed to being the wife God called me to be. I went back to loving, honoring, and respecting my king.

Now, I would be lying to say that once we got over that humungous hurdle everything was peaches and cream. No, we just learned how to fight our battles. When we finally got on one accord, we began to run like a well-oiled machine.

Jewel #3
Kill Your Flesh

"My counsel is this: Live freely, animated and motivated
by God's Spirit. Then you won't feed the compulsions of
selfishness. For there is a root of sinful self-interest in us
that is at odds with a free spirit, just as the free spirit is
incompatible with selfishness. These two ways of life are
antithetical, so that you cannot live at times one way and at
times another way according to how you feel on any given
day. Why don't you choose to be led by the Spirit and so
escape the erratic compulsions of a law-dominated
existence?"
Galatians 5:16-18 MSG

I'll never forget those first months and years after Cort and I got back together. There were still lingering unresolved issues. Our getting back together didn't fix everything that was wrong. If you've ever dealt with a separation from your significant other and you decide to try to make things work, you understand how difficult that is. The time that has passed, the extramarital distractions, all the self-inflicted complications…you don't just automatically bounce back from that.

There are hard conversations that have to take place. Conversations that are littered with confessions and apologies-and that's when the hard work commences. The rebuilding process is grueling and strenuous both emotionally and physically but the reward after its completion is absolutely worth it. I believe the only way to move past the hurt and disappointment is by having relationship with Jesus. The Holy Spirit is what allowed me to pull down destructive thoughts that would rise up.

It was in this season that I knew my prayer life had to go to another level. Prayer should be our automatic response to whatever happens in life. It's in our time of prayer and communion with God that we can release our frustrations, fears, disappointments- anything that may be hindering us from moving forward. Why is this so important? Because when we face difficulty in our marriage, if our automatic response is going to God, He can use that time to supernaturally shift our mindset. Instead of flying off the handle during difficult situations, take a moment, invite God in. Give him your anger, give him your disappointments. In return He can give you peaceful resolution. Now, that peaceful resolution may be in the form of you being quiet.

Sometimes, we allow our unbridled tongues to make situations worse. Something that could have easily been resolved with a little understanding from both parties, could blow up just because we are unable to hold our tongues. I had to learn that every thought I have doesn't have to be expressed. In fact, it's the very thoughts we have in arguments that we should be careful of because once they're out, they're out. It's like trying to put toothpaste back in the tube after squeezing too much. No matter how much we apologize for the things we've said, the effect of those words will linger in the minds of those we offend.

In our prayer time with God, we have to learn how to be honest with ourselves and God. If we can't be honest with God and ourselves we don't have a chance in the world of being honest with our husband. When we learn how to be connected with God intimately, we can allow Him to teach us how to be the perfect help to our spouses.

The greatest thing about being saved is having the Holy Spirit. When you accept Jesus Christ as your Savior, you receive the gift of the Holy Spirit (Ephesians 1:13) and the Holy Spirit has a job. You can be sure of one thing- He will always do His job. One of His jobs is to be our reminder. He leads and guides our decisions. He tells us what to say and what not to say, what's right and what's not right, what's beneficial for our lives and what's simply a distraction. The problem is that instead of obeying the Holy Spirit, we downright ignore Him and choose our own way of "handling" matters.

One of the things I hated about myself is how reckless my mouth was during me and Cort's arguments. I would like to chalk it up to me just being young and immature but it was deeper than that. There was always this voice saying "stop, don't say that". But what did I do? I said it real loud! No matter how much I regretted it after our argument, the same thing would happen the very next time. What was happening? I was giving reign to my fleshly desire to win instead of obeying the Spirit of God.

Why are there so many divorces? Why can't we seem to make it work? Several reasons- one being that when it's time for the vows, some of us made the mistake of just committing to each other and not God. Yeah, we stood up and said "I make this vow in the presence of God and our family and friends…when instead it should be "God I vow to you to be this, do this, and sacrifice this".

It's important to commit to God, because let me tell you, your spouse WILL do something a lot of days to make you want to break every vow you uttered on your wedding day. But committing to God may give you more pause. It should make you rethink packing your bags and giving up.

Another reason is that we as human beings are naturally selfish. We want what we want, when we want it, and how we want it. If someone asked me what the key to my successful marriage is I would tell them that it's killing my flesh every single day. Listen, if marriage is ordained by God (and it is), how can you expect to run it with flesh? It can't be done. Well, it can be done if you both are just content with living mediocre lives based on your own fleshly wants and desires. However, you can expect infidelity, lack of trust- respect- and boundaries. You can expect to be constantly at odds with one another. So when we pray and ask God to heal our marriages, we have to be willing to kill our flesh. Every time we obey God, every time we choose God's way over our own we're killing our flesh.

I remember Cort and I discussing this a few years ago. One of the major "ah ha" moments in our marriage was when we devoted our prayer time to pray specifically for God to change us- our individual selves. My prayer used to be "God, help Cortney to understand his actions toward me, help him to be this and to do that". But when I began to pray and surrender my flaws and inconsistencies to the Master, He changed my entire life. My perspective shifted. Perspective is everything. I began to consume myself with trying to please God and trying to be the best I could be until I had very little time to see Cortney's shortcomings.

See, before, I struggled with admitting fault in myself. I was self-righteous. Admitting I was wrong in any way would mean that a lot of our marriage woes were my fault. I couldn't even wrap my brain around the possibility of me being the problem. But the first step to recovery really is admitting you have a problem or that you are the problem in my case. This doesn't mean that I blamed myself completely or that Cortney didn't have some responsibility. It simply meant that my focus shifted to changing me, which is something that I can control.

You have to learn how to surrender to God the things that you can't change and allow Him to make sense of it for you. You also have to learn how to cover your husband's flaws. Just go ahead and decide, I forgive him for not being A-one in this area and I choose to focus on his strengths. When I did that, the amazing thing is that he began to improve in the areas he lacked in.

Jewel #4

The Power of Agreement

"Again I say to you, That if two of you shall agree on earth as touching any thing that they shall ask, it shall be done for them of my Father which is in heaven."
Matthew 18:19 KJV

Normally when you're having a dispute with someone you automatically know that it's time to put your defenses up. You have to stand your ground and make known your truth, your side of the matter. Well, dispute in marriage is totally different. Your mindset has to be different when you are having a difference of opinion with your husband. I had a terrible habit of rebutting whatever Cort would say. No matter what the disagreement was about, I would get so defensive about it. See, that's the tendency to not be submissive trying to linger around. He could just be trying to suggest a better way to handle a situation and I would immediately get defensive.

I remember plenty arguments starting that way. One day, he just had to sit me down and tell me "look, I need you to understand that I'm on your side. We're on the same team." He said that to me and changed my entire thought process of how to handle disagreements. You will see the word "perspective" several times in this book, because PERSPECTIVE is everything. Having the ability and willingness to shift your mindset is very powerful. When you grasp the principle that "two become one flesh" you can understand that when circumstances arise, it has to be you and him against it. There has to be clarity that what affects him should affect you. So if that is true then what makes him uncomfortable makes you uncomfortable. If he is uneasy about something, it's worth it to have a conversation and work it out. He deserves your consideration and understanding. Talk it out, get to mutual ground and move forward.

Agree to Disagree. We've all heard this said at some point in our lives. Either you've witnessed an argument between others or you've been in an argument with someone and said this. We're quick to say "let's just agree to disagree". Those are words peacemakers utter, you would think. "I'm just trying to keep the peace". I have said it many times before myself.

A few months ago, Cort and I were talking about old times. We were just reminiscing on all the things we've faced and overcome together. As we were talking, the subject of disagreements came up. He said "and yeah, I hate when you say 'let's just agree to disagree', there is no such thing in a marriage." I was like "What?? Yes it is!" He went on to say that in order for our relationship to continue to work and move in a positive direction, we MUST be in agreement. Listen, I completely understand. I know that if two want to walk together they must be in agreement (Amos 3:3). Hey, I get it! I was simply saying that for the sake of an argument we could just agree to disagree on certain things.

Well, that's where the significance of fighting small fires come in. We'll talk about that in a second. For instance, we had this disagreement about me wanting to purchase our oldest daughter a new car for her sixteenth birthday. Whatever she wanted is what I wanted to buy her. We totally disagreed about buying the car. See, Cortney is the, for lack of a better word, "disciplinary" parent. So am I, but more so him. His primary goal is to instill discipline and responsibility in our daughters. He doesn't waver in his approach. I, on the other hand, confess that I am a little too lenient with them at times. I sometimes find it difficult to stick to punishments. I think it stems from my childhood. I didn't get to experience things that other kids my age experienced. I really just want them to have the life that I never had.

Needless to say, we've bumped heads about the severity and length of punishments several times. Anyway, in this instance, he felt that if she had shown the appropriate level of responsibility at that point in life then yes, we'll *think* about getting it. My crazy self said "well, I just want to get it for her because she is our daughter and she deserves the best!" I'm laughing as I'm typing because of how crazy that sounds. But I know I'm not alone in this. Ladies, I know some of you feel me. We want our kids to have the best of everything and will go above and beyond to make sure it happens.

So after going back and forth about this for a while, I got tired of talking about it and said "let's just agree to disagree". Well, when you're married, one thing you don't want to do is disagree about money.

Let me put a pin right here, I'll get back to the car situation in a second. In our household, there is one pot. This may not work for everyone; this is just how we handle our finances. His money is my money and mine is his. We both know how much the other makes and we always discuss how our money will be used. We each have our own savings accounts but we are both in the know when it comes to all financial matters in our home. We decided to do this very early on in our marriage. Listen, if you can't trust him with your money, you can't really trust him with anything. I don't handle the disbursement of money because I'm not disciplined enough. It's not that I'm a big spender, I actually hate shopping. But if my children ask me for anything or want to go somewhere, it's on!

I actually have a personal budget that I live within. I welcome this because I know our family has goals and we wouldn't accomplish them by carelessly wasting money. Ladies, we can't be rebellious when it comes to this. If you know you don't manage money wisely, let him do it.   You'll end up broke, busted, and disgusted because "he can't tell me what to do with my money!" And let me add this, even if you are the money manager, you cannot use that as a way to exert authority over him. He is still the head and should be respected as such. Being the money manager is not a gender specific task. It should be based on who is most qualified to handle that task.

Ok, back to the car situation. So, even though this was not even an immediate concern because we have a few years before she can even drive, we had to find resolution. There has to be some sort of agreement before we move forward. We both gave each other a chance to voice our opinion and we compromised on the best solution for our family. That doesn't mean that circumstances or our opinions won't change to where we have to decide to go another way. But for understanding sake, we agreed on a solution.

Deciding to agree to disagree is a slippery slope of unnecessary marital discord. Agreeing to disagree leads to we're not on the same page. We're not on the same page leads to you do you and let me do me. You do you and let me do me leads to let's just live separate lives. When you start living your life only based on your feelings and wants, you have already condemned your marriage to failure.

If we would've just allowed this issue to be swept under the rug, there would have been consequences attached to not dealing with it on the front end. The power of agreement is absolutely transformational! It causes major shifts in your household when you reach it.

Jewel #5

Fighting the Small Fires

"Hot tempers start fights; a calm, cool spirit keeps the peace." Proverbs 15:18 MSG

It is imperative to fight the small fires at ground level when they arise in your marriage. Small fires are little issues that appear to be harmless in nature but if left alone could cause major damage. A lot of times in our relationship we tend to sweep those little issues under the rug. See, what the enemy loves to do is magnify the small things at the perfect time to make them seem insurmountable.

He chooses the moments we are not necessarily meshing with our husband. Yes, we have those moments when we're not completely in sync. When the smallest things he do irritates us. We all have those moments, and that's totally fine. It's called being married. But the problem lies in our failure to address these small issues. Maybe he did something that really hurt your feelings but you decided, you know what it's all good, I'll let that slide. Or maybe he said something in front of your friends that embarrassed you. That's ok, I'll let that slide. Maybe he's always late when it's time to spend quality time together. It's all good; at least we're spending time.

Listen, the devil doesn't fight fair. He's sitting back waiting for his chance to whisper to you and sow little seeds of discord. "He doesn't respect you at all. He couldn't care less about this date night. You see how Edward treats Bella, that's real love. That's what you deserve". The enemy taunts you with all kinds of disparaging thoughts. But we have to learn to not allow those thoughts to fester. Don't take hold of the thoughts, bring them under subjection.

You don't have to be silent. You can do something about your feelings. What do you do about it? Well, the first thing to do is pray. Then go to your husband and make him understand how this thing affects you. Express the seriousness of it with the hopes that he honors your sincerity and tries to work on it.

We can't control what he does or how he responds but we can control our responses. Most times, the way we respond sets the tone for the type of conversation we'll have. So, don't allow hurt feelings, past failures (on either parts), and stubbornness to hinder reconciliation in that area. If you do, it will lead to loss of time. Time wasted arguing, being upset, or not speaking. That's precious time that could be used to love and make love- to create lasting memories with one another.

Every person in a relationship wants to hear that you love them, need them, and want them in your life. If that is not expressed verbally or emotionally it can cause a disconnection to form. But here's the good news. Having a relationship with Christ teaches us how to have a successful relationship with our spouses. It teaches us how to handle disagreements- be it big or small. I believe the Word when it tells me that when I put God in His rightful place as top priority in my life everything else will fall into its right place. (Matthew 6:33)

That means my marriage, my children, my friendships, my finances-EVERYTHING has to fall into place. So if I'm struggling in any area of my life, my first thought is to check my relationship with God. If I'm struggling to see eye to eye with my husband, I check my relationship with God. Am I consistently studying His Word? Am I spending enough time talking to Him and waiting on His response?

Have I allowed my daily responsibilities to overshadow my need to commune with God?

See, I made a decision to allow the Holy Spirit to guide me so that means I must be obedient to Him. My marriage won't work any other way. Trying to be married without God will leave me DIVORCED. I've already tried it my way. I wasn't able to recognize small fires. And because I wasn't able to recognize them they became combustible situations that I felt couldn't be extinguished.

What I learned is that without God an argument is not just an argument, it's emotional annihilation. With God, I'm able to reject the enemy's instructions and influences. See now, when I misstep, it's the Holy Spirit's conviction that gives me the desire to want to make things right. But what if it's my husband's fault? You're having an argument that you know you are justified in, how can you get your point across and make him understand that he is simply WRONG? God will correct him. And not only correct him, but cause him to come back to you and apologize. That's the benefit of marrying someone who has a relationship with God. You don't have to worry about trying to make them see that you're right and vice versa.

Listen, it has not always been easy for me or Cort to admit we're wrong. There were times we would go without talking for weeks…and that's not an exaggeration! It seems so ridiculous to me now but we had to grow to understand how important it is to not allow things to fester. We've learned the enemy's tricks and schemes. So we have decided that when a disagreement arises, we don't ignore it. We face it head on and move forward. We may digress for a short time to allow cooler heads to prevail, but we never allow it to linger.

Here's the thing, allowing God to be the center of your marriage relieves the pressure off both spouses to fill the void that only true intimacy with God fills. When we learn how to focus on being who we should be and doing what we should do, it leaves less time for you to harp on your husband's mistakes. And the truth of the matter is that probably more times than you would like to admit, you've done something to exasperate the situation. So check your ego at the door and be willing to hear from God. Submit yourself to God's way of resolving matters; even if that means you slithering back in the room and apologizing.

Jewel #6
You Can't Change Him

"And I will give them one heart, and I will put a new spirit within you; and I will take the stony heart out of their flesh, and will give them an heart of flesh." Ezekiel 11:19 KJV

One of the most basic lessons I had to learn, that I honestly already knew, was that I cannot change Cortney Knox. We've heard people say this over and over again. We believe we understand this but our actions reveal otherwise. One of the most common mistakes we make as wives is thinking we are the ones who can change him. Oh, you don't think this applies to you? Ok, so have you ever not done something for hubby because he pissed you off? He said he would come straight home after work but instead decided to go out with the guys. But what he didn't know is that you planned a romantic night for the two of you. Well, since he didn't come home, all of that is out the window. So you take off your sexy lingerie and put on those ugly pajamas. You even figure out some clever, subtle way to let him know what type of night he WAS in for.

In your mind you're saying, next time he'll think about me first! You think by not giving him what he wants you will change his behavior. If I punish him enough by taking away sex then he'll respond the way I want. Listen, that's a risky trick that can quickly and easily back fire! 1 Corinthians 7:5 tells us "do not deprive each other [of marital rights], except perhaps by mutual consent for a time, so that you may devote yourselves [unhindered] to prayer, but come together again so that Satan will not tempt you [to sin] because of your lack of self-control".

So when you try to punish him, what happens is you become more upset and frustrated that he just doesn't get it. He will then feel justified by looking other places to fulfill what his wife is not. Does it excuse his behavior if he decides to cheat? Absolutely not! But the key here is making sure you are doing what you are called to do as a wife. The enemy will worm his way into any crevice you leave open. The saying "don't get yourself out of line trying to get someone else in line" is a perfect way to put it. By trying to change our husband, you are basically saying "I don't trust God to do His job".

If by snapping our fingers we could change our husband into the man we want him to be, we would do it in a second. But because we are flawed ourselves, we would more than likely change him into someone we don't even need for our future. That's why it's best to allow God to mold and shape him and you into who you need to be for each other.

You do know that the feelings and desires you have now will change as you evolve in life? The Bible says that God knows our thoughts from afar and that He is intimately acquainted with all our ways (Psalm 139:1-4). He knows our past, present, and future and nothing will ever surprise Him. Our king being in the hands of the King of kings is infinitely greater than being in our unskilled hands. Allow God to mold you into the wife you need to be for your husband. We don't have the power to change our husband's flaws or shortcomings. We have to live our lives in reverence and accordance with God's Word and trust that our witness will evoke a desire for change in him.

We were at a marriage event and someone asked the question, how do I get my husband to come to church? The speaker said something to the effect of just continue to live your life in front of them. Your witness will compel them to Christ. If they see the change in you, then they will want to experience that as well. I agree. Sometimes after you've had the conversations and have expressed to your husband how you feel but still don't see a change in him, that's an opportunity for you to let your life witness to him.

Now, if you are still doing the same old things and haven't changed how can you expect him to? You're cursing him out and acting crazy but want him to spend more time with you? How? Start responding to situations differently and I guarantee he will see the change.

Jewel #7

The Balancing Act

"And they twain shall be one flesh: so then they are no more twain, but one flesh." Mark 10:8 KJV

Ok, so this is a quick little jewel I picked up along the way. Marriage could be described as a balancing act. After I wrote this chapter, God told me to research the word "balance". The definitions blessed me so much that I knew He wanted me to include it for you. Balance (noun) is defined as "an <u>even distribution</u> of weight enabling someone or something to remain <u>upright</u> and <u>steady</u>". Balance (verb) means "to keep or put (something) in a <u>steady</u> position so that it does <u>not fall</u>". Whew! This blessed me so much! This is how God wants us to view our marriages.

Cortney is the most consistent person I know, which is an area that I struggled in. He says he's going to do something and come hell or high water, he does it. That's one of the things I admire most about him. Me, if I promised you that I would go with you somewhere later that evening, but Mr. Bossman pushed my buttons one too many times that day, oh honey, you would get a cancellation call or text from me real quick.

Before getting married, I never recognized this as a character flaw. I can just imagine how frustrating this must've been for him to deal with. But without verbalizing it, he taught me that your commitment is connected to your integrity and it matters greatly in life.

That's just one of the areas in which he balances me. One day I just sat and thought about the things I have struggled with and how Cort has been the perfect yin to my yang. I'm so grateful. But here's the thing, my lacking in an area doesn't excuse me from desiring to be better. One of the important jobs of being a spouse is not only making up the difference and balancing your union out but it's also helping your spouse develop in their weak areas. Where I lacked in sticking to promises Cort excelled. Instead of him bringing up my problems every chance he got, he simply led by example. Sometimes that's what it takes- you being consistent in an area.

So as spouses, our job at times will be to pick up the slack of the other half so that no matter what season we're facing in our marriage, we will never fall, but always stay upright on steady ground!

Jewel #8

Independent Woman vs. Submissive Wife

"Wives, understand and support your husbands in ways that show your support for Christ. The husband provides leadership to his wife the way Christ does to his church, not by domineering but by cherishing."
Ephesians 5:22-23 MSG

When you are raised to be an independent woman, submission may be a foreign concept. It's hard and doesn't come naturally. My mom was a single mother working sometimes two and three jobs to provide for five children. One thing I'm grateful that she taught me is how to be independent. I remember being so eager to turn fifteen so that I could get a job to help her financially. Although I left home at an early age, because she taught me how to be independent, I was able to sustain some sort of normalcy.

We live in an age where #girlpower and women's rights are all the rage. I love it and I greatly support it! However, we cannot allow our sense of independence and equality to cause us to neglect God's standard for us as wives. Based on God's word for wives, submission is vital to having a successful marriage. Some of you won't like this but here it is anyway.

Genesis 3:16 says "To the woman he said, "…Your desire will be for your husband, and he will rule over you." And here is the most known verse found in Colossians 3:18, "Wives, submit yourselves to your husbands, as is fitting in the Lord."

This can be kind of hard for us wives to accept, especially in this day and time. We can pretty much get everything we need on our own without a man's help so why would we "bow down" to him. Well, I think the Message version of this verse helps bring it all into perspective. It says, "Wives, understand and support your husbands by submitting to them in ways that honor the Master". That sounds better right? Listen, God is such an awesome God, he has a plan and a purpose for each person according to His will. It's not his desire for us to be slaves to any human being, especially our husband. There are certain things that each person is charged to do in order to fulfill God's Word.

Again, our problem most times is that we are so focused on our husband's purpose and how he is not doing it right, until we completely negate what it is that we are supposed to be doing. Why are you so concerned with the speck in my eye when you have a Goliath-sized log in yours? (Matthew 7:4) How much better would this world be if we focused on correcting our own failures instead of judging others? How much more productive would we be?

We have a tremendous job as a wife and queen of our home, one that we should be proud to undertake. We have the privilege of supporting, understanding, building up, and creating peace for our king. We as wives will never be able to truly fathom the amount of pressure men have on them to be the leader of their homes. The weight of him being held accountable for carrying the family on his back through a world that condemns his every move is enormous.

Even if you have a husband who you feel hasn't lived up to his purpose, one who hasn't exemplified kingly qualities-you still have the assignment. How about this? What if instead of you belittling him in your own sly way and affirming his inner insecurities, you began to speak life into him? What if you called forth the leader in him; what if you showed him how much he is needed? What if you devoted yourself to fasting and praying for his triumphant ascent to the place God has called him to occupy? Our job should be our privilege!

Be the queen that God called you to be because you are needed in a major way!

Listen, please don't misconstrue the message in this book. I'm not saying we should be wives who sit in the background and follow our husband's every command. There may be some times in our marriage where we have to make a stand and demand to be heard and respected. What I'm saying is that there is a righteous way to do that. If you are not married yet, here's some advice: pray that God allows your husband to find you. Marry someone who loves God. Even though the first years of my marriage were the toughest time in my life, I could not imagine going through it with someone who is not saved.

Our marriage was restored because of our relationship with Jesus. If you're already married, though, it's imperative that you learn how to be a strong but submissive wife without verbally killing your husband. Even if you married someone who is not saved, please know that the name of Jesus is bigger, greater, and stronger than any circumstance we face. That just means that your husband definitely needs to have a wife who is faithful in obedience to God.

That example could be his saving grace. So don't give up, be encouraged!

Jewel #9

Honoring Your King

"A good woman is hard to find, and worth far more than diamonds. Her husband trusts her without reserve, and never has reason to regret it. Never spiteful, she treats him generously all her life long." Proverbs 31:10-12 MSG

Restoring the significance of the role of Husband in the home is vital. As a woman of God, as a wife, as the queen of my kingdom, I do what is necessary to keep my husband happy and satisfied. Just as Christians who love Christ are inspired to keep His commandments, which pleases Him, that's how we should view our role in our marriage. Your union should be one that you are proud of. How is it going to get to that point? You have to do what it takes to improve your marriage!

I recently ran across a video made by a married couple on YouTube. This just seemed to be a vlog of their normal daily routine. The wife was cooking dinner and she says ok babe let me fix Cheyenne's (I don't remember the baby's name for real) plate and then I'll fix yours. The husband was like naw babe you should fix my plate first and then feed Cheyenne. Immediately they began this huge debate about whose plate should be fixed first. The wife argued that he was completely wrong for even suggesting that he would eat before a starving baby. Now, let me point out that the baby didn't seem to be agitated to the point of needing immediate attention. Anyway, the husband argued that because he was the man of the house, he deserved to be fed first. The debate went back and forth and they asked their followers to comment on who they felt was right in the situation.

I began to think about this. We often make up these illegitimate excuses to justify our unwillingness to be submitted to or honor our husbands. Cheyenne is starving and you want me to feed your overgrown butt first? What kind of man/father are you? Wives, I want you to put your good reading glasses on right here. It is your husband's God-given right to be respected in his home. There are some things that we may feel are ridiculously uncalled for, like fixing his plate before everyone else's. Well, no matter how insignificant we think something is, if that's what your husband sees as a form of respect, why wouldn't you oblige? Putting him first is a way to prove to him that you honor and respect his role in your life. It makes him stand a little taller everyday he leaves home. Why wouldn't you want to be the reason he brims with confidence? Especially if you have a man who works, provides, and cares for his family!

In the wife's opinion, she felt that the baby needed to be fed first instead of a grown man who is capable of waiting longer. She's making excuses for her obstinacy. What she doesn't understand is that his ability to boldly walk in his rightful place as the man is greatly dependent on her ability to allow him to be the man. And even more, the excuse wasn't even valid. The baby was fine. It would've taken her less than two minutes to fix his plate. This is a small thing but most times our biggest issues began with something small that could've been avoided if we had the right mindset. Let's stop creating issues where there are none.

And to just add my whole belief system on who comes first...in my house, Cortney comes before the girls. Let's be clear, this doesn't mean that our girls go lacking for necessities, emotional support, or anything like that just because Cort's wants and needs come first. Listen, children can unintentionally cause rifts in your marriage. They require a lot of attention. Without even realizing it you're spending the vast majority of your time being mom so much so that you neglect your husband.

Being a mom completely takes over your life. That's why it's so important to find a balance.

Putting your spouse first doesn't make you a bad parent. If anything it makes you a better parent. Your children learn from you by watching you live. If mom and dad are not good, the family is not good. Our children's futures and views of life are shaped by how they see us live our lives.

There were some things that I experienced when I was growing up that held me back later in life. It greatly affected my relationships. It's extremely important for your children to see that- to see you honoring and respecting your king and vice versa.

At the end of the day, my life is intertwined with Cortney's. We are one flesh that can't be divided, not even by our children. When our girls go off to college and are found by their husbands, who will be left? Me and Cortney! So that relationship is one that must be nurtured every single day.

Jewel #10
The Social Media Effect

"Don't become so well-adjusted to your culture that you fit into it without even thinking. Instead, fix your attention on God. You'll be changed from the inside out. Readily recognize what he wants from you, and quickly respond to it. Unlike the culture around you, always dragging you down to its level of immaturity, God brings the best out of you, develops well-formed maturity in you."
Romans 12:2 MSG

A quick way to get your marriage off track is by living in the fantasy world of SOCIAL MEDIA! Your desires are shaped by your exposure, right? Ok, if you took an honest assessment of your social media intake, how much time would be wasted on social media? And not just social media but television as well. Now don't get me wrong, I'm not one of those super critics who believe social media is the devil. I like to call them the "Mama Bouchers" of the world. If you don't know who Mama Boucher is, I need you to make a note to google it later and watch the movie. It's hilarious!

Anyway, I believe that social media is a tool. It can either be used for good or evil. But more so than not, it has been used for evil to force unrealistic expectations to constantly be seared into our brains. The worst thing about it is that people are no longer able to recognize what's real and what's fake.

Every relationship has its own struggles; some that you wouldn't even be able to handle. So when you're wishing hubby would take you out more or be as thoughtful as your Facebook friend's husband, remember you don't know their story. Social media stacks on the already towering mountain of our desire for instant gratification. Instant gratification is like kryptonite for a flourishing marriage. Your desire for instant gratification prevents you from putting in the hard work needed for a successful marriage.

Marriage is work! Instead of dealing with your spouse with grace, you'll begin to be frustrated at every mistake he makes and not allow him space to grow. Longsuffering goes out the window because hey, all your Facebook friends seem happy, why can't we be happy? Before you know it you will even start posting false statuses to keep up with the Joneses when in reality, you're living in hell at home.

Truth is, if you spent the time and energy doing what it takes to improve your marriage that you do faking the funk, you'll be living in a marriage full of love and vigor instead of resentment and stagnation. Stop looking at the "posted" lives of everybody on Facebook! IT'S NOT THE WHOLE STORY!! Focus your attention on doing what is pleasing to God and allow Him to beautify your union.

Jewel #11

Victory Lies in the Lesson Learned

"And I will restore to you the years that the locust hath
eaten, the cankerworm, and the caterpillar, and the
palmerworm, my great army which I sent among you. And
ye shall eat in plenty, and be satisfied, and praise the name
of the Lord your God, that hath dealt wondrously with you:
and my people shall never be ashamed."
Joel 2:25-26 KJV

After me and Cortney's reunion, I struggled with forgiving myself. I felt that I wasted so much time. I just couldn't get past the guilt of stealing time away from our family. I had these conversations with God trying to figure out why we had to go through it. My thoughts were haunted by every single disagreement that led up to the separation. Why did I say that? Why did I do that? Should I have taken more time to do this? Every problem we experienced resurfaced and now resided in my head alongside the simple remedies for them. I was mentally tortured by all the shoulda-coulda-woulda's.

Even though those memories also served as a reminder to never go back to that person, I still struggled with forgiving myself for loss time. Time is so precious. We're here today and could unexpectedly be gone tomorrow. But one day God spoke to me. He said, "With me, what seems like defeat is never a defeat but it is instead a victory in understanding". I began to realize that I learned something from this storm! There is no wasted experience with God. Instead of allowing those memories to incite regret, I now use them as motivation to help other wives bypass that route.

When you think about the most challenging season in your life, what do you think? If you're like me, it's a time that you want to hide in the deepest abyss of your mind never to be thought of again. What the enemy would love for us to do is live in our regret, fear, and frustration. It's his goal to make us second guess if we're worthy of the good life God has planned for us. I'm here to remind you that you are. No matter what has transpired in your life, whether it was your fault or not, God is a restorer. If we just allow Him to work those things out for our good, our future can't be compared to what we faced in our past.

God told me my purpose was to minister to young wives in the body of Christ by sharing my testimony. I never knew that what I went through was attached to my purpose. When He revealed that to me I was hesitant to say the least. I thought, "God you know I'm a private person and I don't want people in my business. I don't want to expose my failures for everyone to see." I felt overwhelmed by the thought of people whispering about my shortcomings. But guess what? My desire to be used by God for His glory outweighed any and every one's opinion.

So although I felt unqualified to offer to be the helper and not the helped, I vowed to allow the Holy Spirit to speak through me. He knows the story better than me anyway. He was right there at the beginning. He was there when we messed up the middle, and He is orchestrating the flourishing today. He remembers the things I forced my mind to forget. Even now He is placing things on my heart that transpired that I forgot about. By allowing my failures to be a testimony, I believe some marriage will be blessed. Some wife will come to know and understand her power and worth and realize how important her role as queen is.

Jewel #12

Let Him Cover You

"Likewise, ye husbands, dwell with them according to knowledge, giving honour unto the wife, as unto the weaker vessel, and as being heirs together of the grace of life; that your prayers be not hindered." 1 Peter 3:7 KJV

Have you ever felt like your husband was jealous, insecure, or too over-protective? Could it be that we have the wrong perspective on this subject. Peter addresses the attitude we should assume as it relates to husbands and wives. Husbands are to honor their wives as the weaker vessel. That "weaker vessel" doesn't equate to least valued among the two. I love how the MSG version says it. It simply means that we as women lack some of men's advantages.

Typically, the woman is more emotional. We tend to react to things based on our emotional state where men are more tactical in their responses. They tend to think about things on a bigger scale or see things for what they really are. Speaking personally, I sometimes allow my feelings to distort the harsh reality of a thing. I hate to say it but sometimes I can be naïve to certain things because I want to always see the best in people.

For instance, years ago, I remember Cort came to me one day and told me that I needed to watch this certain individual because his intentions were not pure. I'm a church girl so of course this had something to do with ministry. Anyway, he warned me that one of the brothers was using ministry to get close to me. I got upset and was really taken aback because I didn't feel he was right. I even went as far as to tell him that he was being a little insecure. I knew when someone was hitting on me and the guy was not doing that. He was just being friendly. Cort suggested that I pull back and just try to avoid him. I didn't see how that was possible being that we had to work together for the ministry we were in. I told him I wasn't about to allow him to stop me from doing the work of the Lord. Just crazy! We had several arguments about this situation. "You laugh too much around him". "You know I'm goofy, I laugh at everybody". Back and forth, back and forth. It's funny to talk about it now but back then it was a real issue.

Well, lo and behold, several months later, the brother actually made a move. It was a subtle, testing-of-waters move, but a move nonetheless. I had to go back and apologize to Cort.

Ladies, we have to understand the difference between our husbands dictating to or commanding us and him actually covering us. Me not allowing him to cover me caused unnecessary conflict in our marriage. Sometimes to have a better relationship all we have to do is simply let him be who God called him to be.

The same situation that he was warning me about manifested with a different sister in the church, so evidently this brother's intentions were never pure. Even though I had no desire for that person, Cortney saw it as a distraction and wanted to protect me from it. All I'm saying is "sis, let him cover you!"

Jewel #13

Love is the Sustainer

"Love never gives up. Love cares more for others than for self. Love doesn't want what it doesn't have. Love doesn't strut, Doesn't have a swelled head, Doesn't force itself on others, Isn't always "me first", Doesn't fly off the handle, Doesn't keep score of the sins of others, Doesn't revel when others grovel, Takes pleasure in the flowering of truth, Puts up with anything, Trusts God always, Always looks for the best, Never looks back, But keeps going to the end."
1 Corinthians 13:4-7 MSG

We like to say "he knows what he married", "I was like this when I married him, so I will not change who I am". I've actually heard women and men say this. The problem with this is that it's ignorance that we conform to because we think it justifies our unwillingness to evolve.

Love offers the power your marriage needs in order to continuously be cultivated. The bible says that "love is patient…." God loves us and knows that we need grace daily to cover our transforming from one person to another. It allows us to make mistakes, hopefully learn from those mistakes and eventually transform us into different, better versions of ourselves. Love is what helps us stay when our spouses gain weight, join him in his battle when he goes through a debilitating illness, keep honoring him when he loses his job, keep a cool head when he starts acting just plum crazy! It is love that helps us endure the hard times. When your relationship is built on love, there is nothing that it cannot withstand.

Pastor Che Cowan explained it best in his "God Is Love" sermon. He said that when he married his wife, he told her that he loved her NO MATTER WHAT. That 'no matter what' meant if she cheated, he still loved her. If she stole all his money, he still loved her. He explained that expressing that kind of love to your spouse will actually set them free. When you have a love like that you don't want to do anything to forfeit it so you're inspired to do what it takes to make sure that love always remains. It's called agape. It's the love that God has for his people.

That was so profound to me. Because God loves me that much, it inspires me to do everything I can to express that same love back to Him. Just as in my marriage. I will do what it takes to protect that love, even though there's nothing I could do to extinguish it.

Truth is-when we really come into the knowledge of Christ's love for us. When we really recognize and experience His unwavering, overwhelming, intoxicating love for us, there is no person we won't be able to show love to. Think about the worst thing you have ever done in life. That thing no one else knows about but you and God- He still loves you even in spite of that. Even if you think about horrible things others have done, unfathomable things that they should die for-God still loves them.

So if Christ loves us this much, how can we not love our neighbor and even more so our spouse? There shouldn't be anything that we can't overcome together. I understand there are issues that we feel are irreconcilable. But if the guilty party truly has a repentant heart and wants to make things work, we owe it to God to try to make it work. God is a restorer-He can heal your marriage! He has the power to make all things new. (Revelations 21:5)

<h1 style="text-align:center">Jewel #14</h1>

<h2 style="text-align:center">All Friends Matter</h2>

"Become wise by walking with the wise; hang
out with fools and watch your life fall to pieces." Proverbs
13:20 MSG

The Bible is clear when it speaks about friendship. God did not intend for us to be loners. He intended for us as sisters and brothers to love one another-build each other up. Ecclesiastes 4:9 says "Two are better than one, because they have a good reward for their toil. For if they fall, one will lift up his fellow". The Bible is also clear about the kind of friend we should have. Proverbs 13:20 says this "Become wise by walking with the wise; hang out with fools and watch your life fall to pieces."

I love my friends. We've been friends since kindergarten. Good friends are hard to find so I'm definitely not ending our friendship because I'm married now. Any of that sound familiar? Well, that's how many of us have managed to keep the wrong people in our circle. The truth of the matter is that when you get married there are some major changes that will have to occur. There are some things you just can't do anymore, there are some places you just can't go, and there are some people you just have to let go of.

I'm sure there are rare instances where your single friend decides to respect the fact that you're now a married woman and not invite you to events or places that may not be appropriate. But you really have to take a true assessment of your friend and the effect she has on your marriage. That goes for single friends, married friends whose marriage is in complete shambles (and they don't care), family members-they all must be evaluated.

Let's say your marriage is struggling. How can your marriage get better if you always vent to people who don't speak life in those tough times? You're venting about what hubby did. I mean you're going on and on and on. She allows you to finish and she responds by saying "see I knew he was no good! He's always doing this and doing that. He never puts you first." Oh, this is a good one, "if I were you I would just----".

Not one time in her rant did she offer a different perspective of why he did what he did. Not once did she ask could it have been your fault. If this sounds like your friend I advise you to DISCONNECT immediately. She is toxic to your marriage-to your destiny! While you may feel it is therapy for you to be able to be transparent with your friends about your marriage, it's actually extremely detrimental.

Your friend may think she is being helpful but really she's sowing little seeds of discord, suspicion, and revenge. You should never have a friend you feel so comfortable with that you bash your husband to. If your friend does not push you to respect your king-even when you're upset, if they join in and help you bash him, if they are not calling you out on your mistakes-that's not a friend you should expose your relationship to. Who we need in our inner circle of influencers are intercessors-we need friends who will remind us of what God says about our marriage. We need friends who won't let us die in our anger and frustration but ones who will pray with us and for us.

Another thing is if your husband is uncomfortable with your friendship in any way, that's an issue that has to be resolved. I don't care if you feel like they are a good friend. I don't care if he/she is the nicest, most caring person in the world. You owe it to him to figure out what the issue is and see if it's fixable. If it's not, let them go! Remember, because you are one with your husband, what bothers him bothers you. You have to get on one accord about every relationship you have because no relationship is worth losing your marriage over.

Now, I do believe we all need that one person we can just be ourselves with and just lay it all out to. And God gave you the very best person-your king. Jesus said "wherefore they are no more twain, but one flesh. What therefore God hath joined together, let not man put asunder". Anyone who intentionally or unintentionally comes in your life and causes any disruption in the union God created is in direct violation of His Word. You must learn how to disconnect or like the proverb says, "watch your life fall to pieces".

Jewel #15

Overcoming Hindrances

"And ye shall seek me, and find me, when ye shall search for me with all your heart." Jeremiah 29:13 KJV

Having a successful marriage is a choice, it is not automatic. You have to choose to do what's necessary to have a successful marriage. During this fifteen year journey, I've learned that there are certain major things that kept me from being the wife God called me to be.

Let's be clear, having a successful marriage and you being the wife that you're called to be are synonymous. You may think, "well no, having a successful marriage will only happen if we both are doing what it takes to make this marriage work". I feel you, that's true. It's hard to have a successful marriage when there's only one person working at it. But it's also true that if you are in a struggling marriage, the healing process can only begin once you're able to take an honest look in the mirror. Yes, he may still be out of place and doing his own thing in the beginning. But my life's journey has taught me that nothing ever stays the same. What I know is that if I choose to partner with God, peaceful resolution is imminent. Partnering with God, what does that mean? It means that I decide to follow God's instructions for my role as a wife and allow him to do the rest.

I was always praying for God to help me be a better wife- show me how to change so that I will have a great marriage. In my prayer and study time, I discovered several things that were hindrances. The first thing was my lack of intimacy with God. My marital struggles didn't stem from the fact that Cort and I didn't have enough time together or that we didn't go out on dates enough or that I didn't do everything I should as a wife. None of those were the real culprit. The root of the problem was that I had no relationship with Christ. Having personal relationship with God is the single most important and foundational piece of the puzzle.

In the beginning of me and Cort's relationship, I didn't know Christ on a personal level so everything I did within our marriage was based off my wants and desires. It made it very difficult for me to see past myself to see what God wanted me to do. Relationship with God helped me to be able to accept Cort's role in my life. I began to hear and OBEY God when he whispered things like "listen to him, he's right". It's one thing to read the Bible and hear what the Holy Spirit is saying to you. It's a totally different thing altogether to actually obey His leading.

See, God didn't just give us our kings to love us and make us feel good when we want it and comfort us when we need it. He also gave him to us to help us, challenge us and push us in the right direction. It's easy for us to accept our husband when he's doing the things that make us feel good, things that we can brag to our friends about. Oh, but when it comes to him giving wisdom or insight about something that we never asked his opinion on, then there's a problem. Relationship with God helped me to be able to recognize Him in Cort's words. I began to submit to his authority over me. I was able to do that because I knew that Cortney was submitted to God.

The second hindrance was laziness. Laziness is one that I know a lot of us struggle with. This is a hard one because most of the time as wives and mothers, we tend to be overworked and underappreciated. It seems like we are always being pulled in an hundred different directions. If it's not our husbands, it's our children. If it's not our children, it's our extended family. If it's not family, it's church, work, friends, enemies, neighbors, cats, dogs, elephants!!!!! EVERYBODY and everything wants and needs a piece of you. Because we wear so many hats, we feel justified in our unwillingness to fulfill the needs of our husband. But let me ask something, why is it that our king's needs and wants get placed on the back burner before everyone else's?

The solution for being overworked and burnt out is simply PRIORITIZATION! I was the world's worst at this. I would always complain to Cort about being so tired, not just physically but mentally. I was so drained that by the end of the day I couldn't push myself to get things done at home. Well, I finally reached a point where I was just tired of not being available at home. The Holy Spirit convicted me and I knew I had to put first things first. So I corrected it. I started saying no to some things at church, at work, and with my extended family. I know you're saying, "that's not being lazy, that's just being dog tired from being over extended". Yeah, but let me finish! See what happened was, after I moved the other things out of the way, laziness slithered right in.

Let me tell you about the beginning. So, I married a true country boy whose mama is the closest thing to the Proverbs 31 woman I have ever met. She paid close attention to her family. I love hearing the stories about the things she did for her children when they were little. I wanted to be like that. I wanted to read my babies stories and make them their favorite desserts every night and go out of my way just to make sure my husband had everything he wanted and needed.

Cortney was used to having full course meals every night and being cared for in a certain way. Now, when we got married he didn't hold me to a certain standard as it related to that but I wanted to make sure he felt loved. I would cook every night, iron his clothes, and do pretty much anything he wanted. But somehow life started speeding up and his wants and needs were unintentionally flung out of the side cart.

So when I decided to let go of some of the less important things in life and prioritize my family, you would think that everything would go back to the way they were. Nope! Guess what happened? Laziness reared its ugly head. Some days I wanted to cook and some days I didn't. Oh yeah, sometimes I wanted to have sex and sometimes I wanted to be left alone. I wasn't tired I just didn't feel like it. The time that I had gained freed me up to watch my favorite shows.

I love my shows-Friends, General Hospital, Grey's Anatomy, The Good Doctor, etc. etc.…..

One thing that Cort hated was when I would say I'm going to do something but then get home and either my mood had shifted or the wind blew the wrong way that day so I reneged on what I had previously said. All I wanted to do was come home and wind down by watching my shows.

Listen, we all have those moments where we just don't feel like doing stuff. I get it. But it's the small things that the enemy uses to stir things up. All of a sudden, in your husband's eyes, you're not reliable. I don't know about you but that's not how I want my king to see me. I'm his queen. I am the one who should be there when he can't rely on any other human.

This happens often in our walk with Christ as well. We ask God for things, "God I just need more time with my family. Lord just bless me with more resources and opportunities to be a blessing to others". Then as soon as it's manifested, we get amnesia and go back on our word. The time you wanted is being wasted on self-gratification. Your opportunity to be a blessing just walked past you but the timing was inconvenient so you disregarded them. So wives, we have to be diligent in our homes. Serving our husbands and children should be a priority.

The last hindrance was selfishness. Now, I stand firmly on the school of thought that says everyone has to be selfish at some point in time. I believe that self-care is highly important! I believe you can't pour from an empty cup. There are a lot of other ways to say it but you get the point.

But frankly, the moment you decided to marry your king you gave up your right to the "it's all about me" life. You decided that you didn't want to live this life on earth alone so you chose the life of compromise. People tend to place a stigma on the word "compromise". It's not a bad word. I actually believe it's a beautiful thing. When a man and his woman come together and decide "I want you to be happy just as much as I want myself to be happy. I'm not good if you're not good". That's a beautiful thing. Ladies, that's what it's all about!

Proverbs 31 depicts what type of strength, grace, integrity, and selflessness we are capable of. We just have to accept the fact that our role requires EVERY bit of ourselves. It's not always easy. Some days you may feel overworked and unappreciated. Yes, take your times of rest but you must get back to it. At those times when you feel like giving up just remember that "God is within her, she will not fall" (Psalm 46:5). Nobody can hold your family together like you. Nobody can fit YOUR crown. It's custom-fitted just for you! Don't forfeit your destiny. Take your seat. Straighten your crown. And let's teach younger generations God's way of Being a Queen in the Kingdom.

References

Associate Pastor Che Cowan- God Is [LOVE]
Word of Truth Family Church, Arlington, Texas
https://youtu.be/lQR98JqLY7I

Join our Facebook group:

KINGDOM Wives Club

www.ingramcontent.com/pod-product-compliance
Lightning Source LLC
Chambersburg PA
CBHW061039050726
47592CB00004B/1510

Paul Mason learned the technique of transcendental meditation in 1970 when he visited the Maharishi's *ashram* at Rishikesh after having hitchhiked from Britain to India. He was spurred him to dig deeper into the history of the teaching of meditation, which led to his being commissioned to write up his research, which has since been extensively revised and expanded, and is now available as *'Maharishi Mahesh Yogi: the Biography of the Man Who Gave Transcendental Meditation to the World'*. He has also translated the teachings and life story of Maharishi's master, Guru Dev - Shankaracharya Swami Brahmananda Saraswati - from Hindi and Sanskrit into English.

Paul was given the honorary *sannyasi* name of 'Premanand' at Swargashram in 2000.

Titles by Paul Mason:

Maharishi Mahesh Yogi: The Biography of the Man Who Gave
Transcendental Meditation to the World

The Beatles, Drugs, Mysticism & India:
Maharishi Mahesh Yogi - Transcendental Meditation - Jai Guru Deva OM

Roots of TM: The Transcendental Meditation of Guru Dev
& Maharishi Mahesh Yogi
^

Den Transcendentala Meditationens Ursprung - Turning
Pages
Swedish edition 2017

108 Discourses of Guru Dev:
The Life and Teachings of Swami Brahmananda Saraswati,
Shankaracharya of Jyotirmath (1941-53) - Volume I
~

The Biography of Guru Dev:
The Life and Teachings of Swami Brahmananda Saraswati,
Shankaracharya of Jyotirmath (1941-53) - Volume II
~

Guru Dev as Presented by Maharishi Mahesh Yogi:
The Life and Teachings of Swami Brahmananda Saraswati,
Shankaracharya of Jyotirmath (1941-53) - Volume III

The Knack of Meditation:
The No-Nonsense Guide to Successful Meditation

Dandi Swami: The Story of the Guru's Will, Maharishi Mahesh Yogi, the
Shankaracharyas of Jyotir Math & Meetings with Dandi Swami Narayananand
Saraswati

Via Rishikesh: A Hitch-Hiker's Tale

Mala: A String of Unexpected Meetings

Kathy's Story

The Maharishi: The Biography of the Man Who Gave
Transcendental Meditation to the World
Element Books - First English edition 1994
Evolution Books - Revised English edition 2005
Maharishi Mahesh Yogi - Aquamarin - German edition 1995
O Maharishi - Nova Era - Portuguese edition 1997

Established in Yoga, Perform Action:
Gita Bhavateet; The 'Song Transcendental' of Acharya Satyadas